Even Though
I Walk…

Coping with Bereavement

Jackie Slough

Onwards and Upwards Publishers

Berkeley House,
11 Nightingale Crescent,
Leatherhead,
Surrey,
KT24 6PD.

www.onwardsandupwards.org

Printed in the UK.

ISBN: 978-1-907509-94-0

Graphic design: Leah-Maarit

Photography:

Kate Barry	pp 3, 10, 15, 17, 19, 26, 29, 31, 37, 39, 41, 56, 59, 63
Deborah Butler	pp 20, 33, 34, 42, 45, 46, 56, 59, 63, 51, 55
Alan Slough	cover, pp 9, 25, 52, 64

About the Author

Jackie Slough is first and foremost a Christian, also a wife, mother and businesswoman. She became an author after the suicide of her youngest son Tom at the age of sixteen in 2004. She felt compelled to write the events of the first week after Tom's death – so as not to forget what happened, as there were so many 'God moments' – and continued for the next five years in journal form to capture each event and emotion as the family struggled to find a new 'normal'. She now owns and runs The Old Bakery Tea Room in Stow on the Wold, Gloucestershire with Alan, her husband, and as a couple they speak to various groups about their journey so far.

Acknowledgements

Thanks and praise to God for putting this on my heart and for His constant encouragement in seeing it done.

Grateful thanks to our friend Liz for proofreading time and time again and for so much encouragement each time, and for her generosity so we could publish so much sooner.

Huge gratitude to Kate Barry and Debs Butler for the use of their beautiful pictures to inspire and delight – each of which is available to purchase as a full size print from their websites:

www.katejbarry.co.uk

www.deborah-butler.com

Thanks again to our publishers, Onwards and Upwards. You are a joy to work with, and your faith in me is amazing!

Contents

This book is dedicated to Tom,
as was the last.

If you hadn't taken your life and started us on this
journey, thousands of people would not have been
touched and blessed by our story. I hope you are
proud of what God has enabled us to do.

We miss you more than you know,
we love you so much,
and how we wish you were still here with us.

See you later Tom…

Foreword by Rev. Philip Deller

It was a dark January evening when the phone rang.

I picked it up. It was Jackie. She said, 'Tom's dead!'

My response was 'NO!'

I immediately drove over to Alan and Jackie's house, praying all the way – for Tom; for Alan, Jackie and James; for a miracle.

I had seen miracles in this family before.

I first met Alan and Jackie on the 30th September, 1999, on the first night of our church's Autumn Alpha Course. Since that night I have had the privilege of seeing the whole family – Alan, Jackie then James and Tom – come to be committed followers of Jesus, baptising them all as believers.

Every life saved and transformed by Jesus is a miracle.

Since then we have walked together, laughed together, cried together and mourned together. In the words of Eugene Peterson we have learned together 'the unforced rhythms of God's grace'. (Matthew 11:29, The Message).

I have also had the privilege of walking alongside Alan and Jackie, and James, as they have walked in the valley of the shadow of death. Tom's death, and the circumstances surrounding it, have been and still are a test of faith, hope and love. Through the pages of this book you will see that all three emerge refined, purified... and victorious. Thanks be to God through Christ our Lord who gives us the victory!

In this book Jackie leads us all on a journey through grief. She speaks openly and honestly about her journey. The book is filled with love; it oozes out of every page and will find its way into the heart of every reader.

Through its words and pictures, I believe that this book will be a blessing to everyone: to those who have walked with grief; to those who are still walking with grief; and to those who are walking alongside someone walking with grief.

Rev. Philip Deller
Chipping Campden Baptist Church

Psalm 23

The LORD is my shepherd,

I shall not be in want.

He makes me lie down in green pastures,

He leads me beside quiet waters,

He restores my soul.

He guides me in paths of righteousness for
his name's sake.

Even though I walk through the valley of
the shadow of death, I will fear no evil, for
you are with me;

Your rod and your staff, they comfort me.

You prepare a table before me in the
presence of my enemies.

You anoint my head with oil;

My cup overflows.

Surely goodness and love will follow me
all the days of my life, and I will dwell in
the house of the LORD forever.

Losing Tom, Finding Grace

Our own journey began on Friday 30th January 2004 at approximately 5.30 in the evening, when I discovered our sixteen-year-old son Tom in his bedroom, having taken his own life by hanging. Alan's journey began minutes later as he tried to resuscitate Tom, even knowing it was too late, but doing it automatically. And for James the journey began as soon as he returned from work and walked into a house full of people who shouldn't have had to be there.

Normal life stopped suddenly then; everything that we had known as safe and standard for our lives was torn away. We had to learn to build a new 'normal' for three instead of four. Alan remembers standing in Tesco early on the Saturday morning (buying milk?!) wanting to scream at everyone who was going about their normal weekly shopping, that our lives had shattered and didn't they know?

We are Christians. As a family we became Christians in 2000 so we each had a faith when Tom died, but our faith is so much stronger now. We have had to lean on the love of God, on His strength and His grace for us as we have walked the walk of grief. We have learnt so much – what to do, what not to do, how to feel, how not to feel, how to respond to others, what to say when friends don't know what to say to us.

This book is a result of that journey and is a helping hand to others starting out on the same road, or for those who want to understand what it is like so they may help their friends or family. It is simply what we have found and experienced or learnt along the way. Sometimes I think, 'Who am I to write a book about grief?' but I am someone who has lived it – is still living it and always will for it is a life journey, not something you ever 'get over' nor should it be.

It is a book biased towards suicide victims because that is our story, but I have learnt that grief is grief no matter what the circumstances and its pain is still very real to all those experiencing it.

I pray you will be blessed, encouraged, lifted up and strengthened by reading this book. If you know Jesus then I pray you may know Him a little more by the end. If you don't, then I pray that you will see something of His love for you – for everyone – that will start you on a journey of discovering that He is who He says He is, that He loves you and died for you so that you might know Him and have eternal life. But even for those with no faith at all I pray that this book will be a help, you will know the things you experience are normal for the different stages of grief and you will be encouraged to journey on, knowing you do not journey alone.

This book has been designed as a guide. The photographs are not there as 'pretty pictures' but are designed to assist you in looking deeper into the interpretation of the picture, leading to meditation on the written words.

How...?

How do you give when you're empty inside?
When your heart is broken and there's nowhere to hide.

How do you love when the feelings have gone?
When you're numb deep inside and can't carry on.

You look to the Lord who is there by your side,
Take your eyes off yourself and in His love abide.

His grace is sufficient for all that you need,
His word is a comfort and the truth you must read.

So look to your Lord when you're empty inside
And He'll carry you on, for you He'll provide.

Death is…

Death is not extinguishing the light;
It is putting out the light because the dawn has come.

You can shed tears because he has gone,
Or you can smile because he has lived.

You can close your eyes and pray that he'll come back,
Or you can open your eyes and see all that he's left.

Your heart can be empty because you can't see him,
Or you can be full of the love you shared.

You can turn your back on tomorrow and live yesterday,
Or you can be happy tomorrow because of yesterday.

You can remember him and only that he's gone,
Or you can cherish his memory and let it live on.

You can cry and close your mind,
    be empty and turn your back,
Or you can do what he'd want;
    smile, open your eyes, love and go on.

Be gentle with yourself

Initially you will be overwhelmed by what has happened. The suddenness of it can be bewildering, and you may feel as people take over, in professional and practical ways, that you have lost control of your life. That's okay – go with it. If it is friends and family, allow them to take care of you; if professionals (police, medics, etc.) allow them to do their jobs. For me, practicality kicked in and I kept everyone topped up with tea and hugs. That's my response to a crisis situation or bad news – to be practical and think practically, what needs to be done, what can I do, etc. – and I guess that is the same for a lot of people, so let them help.

I was comforted by a poem that taught me that the grieving process takes time. It is a long journey, one we wish we were not on and which we would not choose, but we are on it nevertheless.

> Do not hurry as you walk with grief,
> It does not help the journey.
> Walk slowly, pausing often;
> Do not hurry as you walk with grief.
> Be not disturbed by the memories that come unbidden,
> Swiftly forgive;
> And let Christ speak for you – unspoken words,
> Unfinished conversations will be resolved in Him.
> Be not disturbed.
> Be gentle with the one who walks with grief,
> If it is you,
> Be gentle with yourself.
> Swiftly forgive;
> Walk slowly, pausing often.
> Take time, be gentle, as you walk with grief.[1]

---

[1] Adapted from a passage in David Elginbrod by George MacDonald.

Talk to God

If you are a Christian then you know God and you know how big He is. He created the universe.

Isaiah 40:26
Lift your eyes and look to the heavens; who created all these? He who brings out the starry host one by one, and calls them each by name. Because of his great power and mighty strength, not one of them is missing.

Psalm139:13-14
For you created my inmost being; you knit me together in my mother's womb. I praise you because I am fearfully and wonderfully made.

Psalm 46:10
God is our refuge and strength, an ever present help in trouble. Therefore we will not fear, though the earth give way and the mountains fall into the heart of the sea.

I think the unexpectedness of a death feels just like that…

Psalm46:1-2
Be still, and know that I am God.

God is big and He cares for you! I truly believe that God doesn't cause the bad things in our lives – His plans are to prosper us and not to harm us (Jeremiah 29:11). Death is a fact of life. We are all going to die; there's no getting away from it! It's just that some die sooner than we expect, in ways we don't expect: illness, suicide, murder or accident.

God knows your pain; He feels it with you. He understands your frustrations, and He is big enough to cope with your anger – even directed at Himself. If venting your feelings at God helps you to release those feelings that you might otherwise direct towards others that you love, then shout away! God won't stop loving you.

You cannot escape His love, nor can you earn it by doing noble and worthy things in His name. The fact is, He loves you – it's as simple as that!

Give permission for people to talk

It is a strange thing (or maybe just a British thing) that we don't know what to say to someone who has suffered the death of a loved one. I know of people whose 'friends' have crossed the street rather than come face to face, to protect themselves from the embarrassment of not knowing what to say – indeed, it happened to us. If you are the grieving person, you may find you have to be the one to initiate conversation, especially about the person whom you have lost, but this gives permission to others by putting them at ease and opens up the conversation. I clearly remember feeling quite miffed at having to do this, but it is something we learnt early on. Also, I struggled with other mothers' weeping and wailing because my son had died, but again I learnt to deal with it and embrace them in their need. I sometimes felt I was giving them what they should have been giving me!

Alan and I have always maintained openness about what Tom did. We travel the country, speaking to groups about our journey and how we have coped – or not! We sometimes invite questions from the floor at the end of our talks, and we always say that there is no question we will not answer.

If you are able to be that open with friends, they will be much more open with you and will be able to support you better. You will also find that there are some people you will naturally not share so much with, people who just want to know you are okay and not to know how you are really feeling, because they can't deal with it.

You will quickly find out who is who, and who you can be real with, and they are the ones who will stick by you, who will listen and not judge you, cry with you and be there for you.

Proverbs 17:17
A friend is always loyal, and a brother is born to help in time of need.

Holding on to the pain

As time went on after Tom died, I found myself holding on to the painful memories, especially those of the immediate time when we found him and dealt with all that. It somehow seemed to keep him alive in my head; I worried that I had forgotten what he looked like – if he stood in front of me, would I recognise him? It sounds silly, but holding on to the hurting kept him alive in my memory.

We learnt, on the first anniversary of his death, because of something written on a card given to us, to see that every anniversary, birthday or Christmas is a step closer to seeing him again and that when we do, the manner of his death, the unanswered questions and unfinished conversations will not be important; they will pale into insignificance compared to the joy that we will experience face to face in the light of Jesus' love.

I believe that God is with us in death as in life. For the true Christian, death is welcomed as going home to be with the Lord for eternity. If our loved one had that faith in life, then we can be assured of where they have gone in death, and there is an enormous amount of peace to be gained from that knowledge. Right from the outset of finding Tom dead, we knew a peace that we had never known before, and a certainty that he is with Jesus and that we shall see him again. It doesn't stop the hurt, it doesn't make the pain go away, but it does make it easier to bear.

I believe wholeheartedly in a God of grace and a God of forgiveness. I believe that God will judge us, but He will judge us with grace, mercy and love. If you do not know if the person you lost had a faith and so you do not have the assurance in your heart that they will be in heaven, then trust completely in God's grace for everyone, and trust that you will only know they are safe in heaven when you get there too. For now, only God and your loved one know, and it is not helpful to your journey to worry unnecessarily. This may be a simplistic view, but it is one that heals, not harms.

Proverbs 3:5
Trust in the Lord with all your heart, and lean not on your own understanding.

It has to be said, also, that if your loved one made a conscious decision to reject God/Jesus throughout their life and they were open about that, then they will not be in heaven. Jesus clearly states:

Matthew 10:32
Whoever acknowledges me before men, I will also acknowledge him before my Father in heaven. But whoever disowns me before men, I will disown him before my Father in heaven.

Mark 16:16
Whoever believes and is baptised will be saved, but whoever does not believe will be condemned.

However, it is still a fact that we do not know what goes on between a person and God at the moment of death. Remember the thief on the cross to whom Jesus said, 'Today you will be with me in Paradise'? The thief recognised Jesus for who He was and openly acknowledged Him, whilst the other criminal hurled insults and abuse at Jesus. Surely it is better to put our trust in that which we cannot see or understand (which is what faith is – Hebrews 11:1) than to worry and fret for the rest of our lives about that which we can do nothing about. It is better to live our own lives in the light of God's forgiveness and grace for us.

Jesus said:

John 11:2
I am the resurrection and the life. He who believes in me will live, even though he dies, and whoever lives and believes in me will never die.

Do what is right for you

Well-meaning people will give you all sorts of advice on how to deal with life after a death. You may feel – as we did – pulled in different directions, given too many choices, too many decisions, and you may feel that it would be rude not to do what people are expecting or asking you to. Even a simple dinner or lunch invite would throw us into a quandary, especially if there were two invites for the same day! We learnt to go with our hearts, our gut feelings, and to go where we felt 'safe', where we could be ourselves, where our hosts would not pressure us for conversation but just love us for who we were and how we were feeling. So trust your instinct; don't worry about offending those who have invited you out – if they love you they will understand.

Don't be afraid to have a good time, to enjoy yourself. I remember the three of us walking down the high street in the days before Tom's funeral, and we were laughing and sharing a joke. I remember thinking, 'What if someone sees us laughing? They'll think we didn't care about Tom.' I felt guilty in that moment for laughing in public, but actually it was a good thing to do – a natural thing – and we shouldn't stop living just because a loved one has died and our hearts are broken.

When it comes to celebrating or remembering your loved one's birthday or the anniversary of their death, and events such as Christmas or Easter, Mother's or Father's Days, do what feels right for you, not what you think is expected of you by others. It is your grief, your pain, and no-one has the right to tell you how to express it. We found – and still do – that we prefer to do things as a family together: Alan, James and I. We place flowers on Tom's grave, and then we will go out for a meal, sometimes taking an 'honorary' fourth person – one of our friends or a friend of James – and we will sometimes raise a toast to Tom or just simply remember him quietly in our hearts.

It took a while for us to make a new Christmas for ourselves, for us to be comfortable as three and not four. It really helped us to focus on the reason for Christmas – Jesus – and to make the day a celebration of His birth rather than to focus on the gap left by Tom.

Family gatherings can be difficult; there will always be one less person there. Try to encourage family members to talk about the person who has died. You may have to be the one to instigate this as they may be afraid of hurting your feelings by bringing the person up in conversation. Try to be natural and not forced, but if the occasion has passed and no-one has mentioned your loved one or asked or acknowledged how you are coping with the day, then be gracious. If you are hurting because of the lack of acknowledgement, then either gently mention that you would have appreciated some comments/conversations, or simply let it go and love the family anyway. Trust that each gathering will get easier, but know in your heart that you will always keep the space open, even if others close it off.

If you are a family member reading this, please, for the sake of the person who has died and the person who is grieving, keep the memory alive. Talk about the deceased, acknowledge the gap at the table, because for the grieving person, or family, it can be upsetting or distressing to have repeated family gatherings with no acknowledgement of the person who has died or the feelings that such gatherings can bring upon the grieving – even after numerous years. It can feel that the person was never there, is forgotten, is literally dead and buried.

Understand Others' Grief

We realised quite early on that we each felt the loss of Tom differently. A mother's grief is different to a father's grief, and a sibling's grief is different to a parent's grief. They are all different according to the natural bond that each had with the deceased. James was very angry with Tom for different reasons. He could see the pain that Tom had caused us. And he was angry because at nineteen and sixteen they were just beginning to really get on and enjoy each other's company, and Tom ruined that. Alan and I felt the loss differently. My grief was very emotionally driven – my flesh and blood that I had given birth to and nurtured for sixteen years. And Alan's was more logically driven – how to support and fix his remaining family whilst dealing with his own grief.

The important thing is to keep communicating, keep talking, but above all understand that you react differently and embrace it. I think we spent some time treading on eggshells around each other, so that we wouldn't upset each other and to try to protect ourselves from any more hurt, but that isn't always the best way. Be open and honest with each other (and yourself) about how you feel, and don't condemn each other but accept each other's thoughts and feelings without judgement.

John 11:33-36

When Jesus saw her weeping, and the Jews with her also weeping, he was deeply moved in spirit and troubled. "Where have you laid him?" he asked, "Come and see, Lord," they replied. Jesus wept. Then the Jews said, "See how he loved him!"

Write it down

It is a really good idea to keep a diary or a journal as soon as possible after someone has died. I felt very soon after Tom died that I should write down all that had happened in the first week – from finding him, to his funeral and Thanksgiving service – so that we would not forget anything. That quickly became a journal that told of our journey, where I poured out my heart to God and to Tom in the form of poems, and where I recorded the events that happened, as our lives took a different turn. My journal became a book – 'Losing Tom, Finding Grace'[2] – but that doesn't have to be the case. It is just good to be able to look back over the things you have recorded and see how far forward you have come, when you think you have only been treading water. Also you can vent your frustrations, fears and other emotions onto paper, which gets them out of your head and is a good part of the healing process, especially if no one else gets to read it. It comes back to the old saying, 'better out than in' – 'in' can damage you but 'out' can heal.

If you have unresolved issues with the person who died – maybe a sibling or a parent – and you never got to say what was on your heart for that person, it is a really good idea to write a letter straight from your heart and to 'post' it in a symbolic way. We know people who have done this and it has been both a comfort and a release for them. If you have the time before the funeral, you can lay it in the coffin – obviously with the knowledge of everyone involved. If it is weeks, months or even many years later that you write your letter, it is important to your healing to say what needs to be said. If you have negative issues, include them in the letter but end the letter on a positive note. A good way to 'post' your letter is to simply burn it, but do this in the company of someone who has supported you throughout your journey. You could then scatter the remains of the letter at the grave if you felt the need.

---

[2] Published by Onwards and Upwards Publishers (2011)

You know how I feel

People who are experiencing grief will expect you to know how they feel, and they will tell you so. But the circumstances of grief are all different, according to how the loved one has died. Ladies who lost husbands thought I would know how they were feeling, but I still had my husband by my side so how could I possibly know their pain? To lose a child through stillbirth or miscarriage is nothing like losing a child to cancer; which is nothing like losing a child to suicide, where they have chosen death; which is nothing like losing a loved one to a fatal accident or by the hands of a murderer, etc. The loss of a parent is equally traumatic, even though we expect our parents to die before us. Sometimes, even when a death has been expected and can be a relief, we can be filled with guilt at that relief. I am not belittling the pain of loss, simply stating that each loss is so different, depending on the circumstances that led to the loss.

I am ashamed to say that until I had experienced the loss of a child myself, I had little or no empathy for those that had – even less if it was a miscarriage – but now I know the pain of a life cut short and dreams and aspirations longed for but unfulfilled. So you can empathise with others in their pain, but it is not your pain, and your pain is not theirs. The grief journey is similar for everyone who is on it – there are common stages that we will all go through at some time – but we will all deal with it in our own ways. My answer to the 'You know how I feel' statement is to gently say, 'Actually, I don't know how you feel – I haven't lost my husband – but I do understand grief, and I understand your pain.'

Loving the living

After Tom died, I struggled with so many emotions, but as the months went on I found it especially hard to continue to love James. I didn't love him any less, but he was not Tom – and it was Tom I wanted. I almost resented the fact that James was alive and Tom was gone, as if, had it been the other way round, it would have been easier; but actually it would have been just as horrid. Your mind will play all sorts of tricks on you in the midst of grief: if you end your own life, it will somehow bring the lost one back, or certainly bring you together again. This is a totally normal feeling and it will go, but do share it with someone close. I know I loved James as much as ever and needed him more than ever, but it was still Tom I wanted and only time could change that.

In the early days I really panicked if James was home late. I imagined the worst – that he had been killed in a car crash. I was just waiting for the knock on the door... Also, if we came home and called up the stairs and he didn't hear us and shout back, then I would instantly assume he had done the same as Tom. In those circumstances I could not bear to go up the stairs; Alan would have to go. I have to admit to still having those feelings, but I think any mother worries about their child for the rest of that child's life, and I have learnt to trust that even should the worst happen, God will carry us through as He has before.

Re-visiting emotions

Over the course of the months following Tom's death, and indeed even years after, we noticed that thoughts and emotions that we thought we had dealt with would jump up and hit us and hurt us all over again, always without warning. We read a book[3] which detailed this, as the authors had experienced the same.

It is quite natural to experience an aspect of grief, work through it and think, quite rightly, that you have dealt with it and moved on, only to find it comes back to hit you at an unexpected time in the future with more force than you felt the first time! The two authors describe it as a spiral staircase, that as you move through life (and grief) travelling upwards on the spiral, you will revisit experiences that you have had, but you will see them from a different perspective. It is natural to try to beat yourself up – as I did – thinking, 'I've dealt with this so why does it hurt now?' but understand that it is all part of the natural process of grieving and it is okay. Once you have done that, it becomes easier, and you welcome the experiences almost like old friends, knowing that you will overcome this time as you have before.

---

3 'Finding Your Way after the Suicide of Someone You Love', David B Biebel & Suzanne L Foster; published by Zondervan (2005)

Wasted years

It is hard to cope with the loss of anyone you love, but if that loss is a younger life it is especially difficult. For me, it is hard when we have the first few days of spring sunshine in February, the promise of warmer days and new life, and I feel the loss of Tom more keenly – if only he could have held on, if only we could have talked, we could have got through... But I know nothing would have made any difference. As his mum, I had so many hopes and dreams for Tom's life (as I do for James) but they are all fruitless – all the ambitions, all the things he could have done or been, all cut dead by what he chose to do. These feelings soon pass as you get on with your own lives. But every sunny day in February, for me, they resurface; they don't cause me any hurt, just a sense of sadness that soon passes.

A new normal

The trauma of losing a loved one in sudden circumstances is huge and has far-reaching consequences. For us, our normal four became an abnormal three, and we had to adjust to that. There are obvious examples: walking into a restaurant and asking for a table for four, setting four places at the table, noticing how food is packed in twos or fours, rarely in threes!

It was sometimes difficult to cope with the normality of other people's lives compared to the destruction in our own. Often I wanted to shout/scream, 'Stop the world! I want to get off!' It felt like all around us was calm in the midst of our chaos, like we were spinning out of control; although outwardly we seemed okay, a bit like the duck swimming calmly on the water but paddling like crazy underneath.

We found a new normal – and it felt good. It didn't feel like we had left Tom behind or forgotten him; we simply kept going as a family of three, that once was four, and it got easier one day at a time. I have found more joy than before in the simple things: flowers, birds, sunsets and the clear, starry sky. I used to enjoy these things, to admire them in a passing glance sort of way, but now I love them. I take time to enjoy them. I am enchanted by them and I see God in all of them. I see His hand in all creation and I see His hand on each of us. It fills me with joy that in all our hurting, God never once left our sides. Even when we couldn't see Him or hear Him or even acknowledge His goodness to us, He never once left us. He never grew tired or weary of our grieving and the silly thoughts and doubts that we had; He just held us securely in the palm of His hand until we could stand on our own feet again – and He will do the same for you.

Isaiah 40:28-31

Do you not know?
Have you not heard?
The Lord is the everlasting God,
The creator of the ends of the earth.
He will not grow tired or weary,
And his understanding no-one can fathom.
He gives strength to the weary
And increases the power of the weak.
Even youths grow tired and weary,
And young men stumble and fall;
But those who hope in the Lord
Will renew their strength.
They will soar on wings like eagles;
They will run and not grow weary,
They will walk and not be faint.

Thorns

Alan and I attended a seminar on grief. At the start we were each given a large rose thorn which represented loss. We were encouraged to hold it for a few minutes and then place it in a pair of carved wooden hands at the front of the room. As I held my thorn, I kept jabbing myself on my fingers as I listened to the speaker. Most of the time it didn't hurt at all, but every so often it really pricked me and was quite painful. It occurred to me that grief is so like that; over time the pain diminishes and then every so often it will catch you unawares and really hurt – maybe just a memory, maybe a song on the radio, maybe a child who looks like yours... Who knows when it will happen, but it surely does and it's okay to go with it. It's not self-pity; it is normal and healthy. If you shed a tear, or a bucketful out aloud, or in your heart, it's okay. You are not falling backwards but moving forwards, and this pain too will pass.

Another strange thing about grief is that as you move further away from the death the pain seems to intensify. You would think that three or four months on it would hurt less, that you would 'be over it by now' but we found it got much worse before it got better. We missed Tom more as time went on, and at times the pain of missing him was unbearable. This does pass, it is normal – but it is horrid.

We found the same with the anniversary of his death – the first was awful, none of us knew how to cope with the day, but I would say that the fifth anniversary was harder, being a significant anniversary. As we approach the tenth anniversary, again being significant, it seems even more like the first, like yesterday... We speak to many parents who have lost a child, sometimes over twenty or thirty years ago, and they all say the same thing: it still hurts.

Some people seem to sail through the grief process; they seem to move on with their lives really quickly. This doesn't mean they loved their lost one any less, but it just shows how the journey is different for everyone.

Depression

This is something you need to address and seek proper medical help for. I ignored the feelings of depression that I felt in the months after losing Tom, telling myself I was alright, even though I would spend days just staring out of the window unable to move. As soon as Alan or James came home, I reverted to myself and did the normal, wifely/motherly things, but on my own I did not function. For me things came to a head when I had a breakdown the following year and battled my own suicidal thoughts. I had to seek medical help and take antidepressants which I had fought against for so long, even working together with my G.P. but maybe not being one hundred per cent honest with him.

All I can say is, if you feel you can't cope, if you feel worthless, guilty, ashamed, if you wish you were dead or even simply restless and fidgety, like you could run forever and still keep going, please go and seek the proper medical help. There is no shame in it. No-one will judge you or think you weak, but ultimately it could save your life.

Matthew 11:28

Come to me all who are weary and burdened, and I will give you rest. Take my yoke upon you and learn from me, for I am gentle and humble in heart, and you will find rest for your souls. For my yoke is easy and my burden is light.

You will laugh again...

The saying that time is a great healer is so true. But in the shock and numbness of immediate grief you will not want to hear it (and anyone who says it to you is unkind and unsympathetic) and you certainly will not believe it. However, it *is* true, and in time you will see it for yourself.

I find I have joy back in my heart. I can laugh, share a joke even be very quick-witted and funny myself. In the early days you may feel guilty for laughing when you think you should be sad, but laughter is a good medicine – God-given medicine for our souls – and we should embrace it and let it happen. (If you find you are cackling hysterically at things no-one else finds funny, I think you should very quickly seek medical help before you are carried away in a straitjacket!)

Psalm 30:5,11
Weeping may remain for a night, but rejoicing comes in the morning ... You turned my wailing into dancing; you removed my sackcloth and clothed me with joy, that my heart may sing to you and not be silent.

Psalm 147:3
He heals the broken-hearted and binds up their wounds.

Forgive Yourself

This is a tough one. We can feel full of guilt when someone we love dies. We should have said or done this or that, not let them go out, been there for them, seen it coming, etc. – the list is endless. In the event of a death by suicide, the guilt is even greater.

Alan and I decided at the outset not to do the guilt trip. It wouldn't bring Tom back, and would only hurt us. I found it easier to say than do, and I did struggle with enormous feelings of guilt – as Tom's mum I should have known and acted on my gut feelings instead of ignoring them. Our church ran a course which dedicated a whole morning to forgiveness: firstly forgiving others and then forgiving ourselves. I found this so hard, but once I had done it and said aloud, "I forgive myself," in the hearing of others, a huge amount of healing was able to take place in me that wouldn't otherwise have happened. If you have issues with someone who has wronged you (abused, bullied or violated you in some way) you need to forgive them – not forget, but certainly forgive.

I strongly urge you, if you are struggling with guilt or you need to forgive someone, to seek help through counselling, with the support of your church or simply with someone you trust; to talk through the issue and to lay it down; and to say clearly, "I forgive myself [or the person who has wronged you]." You may say it through many tears, as I did, but say it aloud. It is so empowering, whereas the guilt is so debilitating. It is good also to write down somewhere that you have done this so that in the future, should doubts strike you (as they may), you have that written confirmation of what you did in the presence of other people.

Romans 8:1
Therefore, there is now no condemnation for those who are in Christ Jesus.

Church

When Tom died, Alan, James and I had no hesitation in returning to church. Tom died on Friday evening, and we were at church on Sunday morning. Where else would we go; to whom else would we run? But I know that for some people that is the last thing they would want to do. They may feel judged or embarrassed or just simply overwhelmed at the thought of facing so many people.

I did struggle more as time went on. I felt embarrassed by my tears. I wasn't convinced that God was there. I felt envious of people who were free in their worship and full of the joy of the Lord – it was all right for them, their world hadn't ended. But I kept going. It would have been so easy to have stopped, but what I came to realise was that God was there, and to worship Him through my pain, hard though it was, was the best thing I could do. He hadn't changed. He hadn't caused Tom to take his life. His love for me was the same as it always had been, and to worship Him was a choice I had to make on a weekly basis. God never once let go of us as a family – how could I not worship?

Even now, after nine years, sometimes that is a choice and decision I have to make – to worship in spite of my feelings, to lift my hands in worship even if I don't feel like it – because God is still God and He deserves our praise. To raise our hands in worship is simply an outward expression of the inward love we have for Jesus, and if we love Jesus with all our heart how can we not raise our hands in worship?

One lady told us that after twelve weeks her church family, minister included, told her, 'You should be over it by now.' It is fair to say that if your church is not supportive then you should consider moving to a church that *does* love and support you and will not judge you. Remember, grief is a life journey, not something you 'get over'. That is not to say, however, that you should milk the sympathy vote. We should learn to overcome, but we are all different and some will overcome quicker than others.

I wrote the poem below in 2009, describing how I felt in church at that time.

Sacrifice of Praise

Why am I here, why did I come?
I need to stay, but I want to run.
I can't face my friends – I just want to hide;
I've nothing to give and I'm empty inside.
I feel so helpless, so weak and so small,
The words of the songs cause tears to fall –
Silently, discreetly so no-one can see
The pain I am feeling – why's it just me?
Everyone else is joyful in praise;
My arms feel like lead – too heavy to raise.
My eyes are downcast, fixed on myself;
I'm drowning in sorrow above all else.
But God is still God, He knows my need,
And Jesus still died – gave His life up for me,
And little by little as I look to His face
I'm lifted right up and bathed in His grace.
I can lift up my voice, my heart and my hands,
Surrender forever my life to His plans.
I'm lost in His beauty, His peace and His love;
I'm lifted in wonder to glimpse heaven above,
To worship my Father, my Saviour, my Lord,
To soar in His presence, as free as a bird.
For this I was born, for this I was made –
I'm so glad I came, I'm so glad I stayed.

Marriage

It is a sad statistic that most couples who lose a child will divorce at some point in the future, if not the near future. Men and women grieve differently. Women are emotional and need to talk about the child, the death, the funeral, anything and everything concerning the situation. Men do not feel the same; they internalise everything and deal with it on a completely different level. This can come across as uncaring, especially if they bury themselves in work or find extra to do. It doesn't mean they don't care; it's just their way of coping.

If you are a couple going through bereavement, then learn the different ways and learn to support each other in those ways. We found that some days I would be up whilst Alan was down, so I was able to support him, and vice versa. Sometimes we would both be down on the same day, in which case we just held and supported each other and didn't expect anything of each other, knowing that tomorrow was another day and that 'this too will pass'.

You do have to make a conscious decision to work at supporting each other, to not apportion any blame to one another, to love each other no matter what. Some days it will be hard, but your marriage is worth fighting for. There came a time, about four years after Tom died, that I felt I didn't love Alan at all. I was on the point of walking out of our marriage, but I realised that, for me, marriage was God-given. I had said my marriage vows before God in church, and to walk out would hurt Alan and James so much and really would achieve nothing. I can honestly say that I love Alan more now than at any time in our thirty-one years of marriage, and I am so proud of him and the way he has held himself since Tom died.

Matthew 19:4-6
Since they are no longer two but one, let no-one separate them, for God has joined them together.

Anger

This is not something that I personally felt, except for a brief moment when I was having a pity party, feeling very sorry for myself, and I said to Tom, 'Look how you have made me feel.' I quickly realised that this was a selfish, indulgent thought, and how much anguish Tom must have been in and wrestled with for such a long time without us noticing. How could I be angry with him for causing me pain when his was so much greater?

But I do understand and accept that anger can and does form a great part of the grief journey for many people. There can be anger towards the one who has died (especially with suicide). How could you leave me like that? Why could you not tell me? There can also be anger towards the person or thing that caused the death: illness, murder, the driver of the other car, etc.

It is right to feel anger. It is a natural feeling and very much part of the grieving process for most people, but not all. The question is how you deal with the anger, how you overcome it without it overcoming you. The danger is that without the right help, you can become very bitter towards your loved one or others, and that can last for years.

If your anger is righteous anger – your loved one died at the hands of others, through neglect or violence – then channel the negative anger into positive by becoming a force for good to get the justice required or to set up a charity or trust to change the future for others, or simply just to use your story to help others. This is easier said than done, I know. But with help – through your doctor or counselling or other self-help groups led by people who have been through the same or similar experiences – your anger will dissipate, and you will eventually find an inner peace that will enable you to come to terms with what has happened.

Ephesians 4:26 (The Message)
Go ahead and be angry. You do well to be angry – but don't use your anger as fuel for revenge. And don't stay angry. Don't go to bed angry.

Worry

It is easy to worry – about the future, about your family, about events that have to take place when someone dies, such as an inquest into the cause of death, to worry about what other people think of us or of the one who died. I know I did my share of worrying. To be honest, I still do… until I remember that I cannot change one thing by worrying about it; all I will do is make myself ill. So I take one day at a time, sometimes one *hour* at a time, and keep putting one foot in front of the other and trusting that the situation will be resolved or dealt with in God's time and by His grace.

1 Peter 5:7
Cast all your anxiety on Him, because He cares for you.

Psalm 121
I lift up my eyes to the hills –
Where does my help come from?
My help comes from the Lord,
The maker of heaven and earth.
He will not let your foot slip –
He who watches over you will not slumber;
Indeed, he who watches over Israel will neither slumber
nor sleep.
The Lord watches over you – the Lord is your shade at
your right hand;
The Sun will not harm you by day,
Nor the moon by night.
The Lord will keep you from all harm –
He will watch over your life;
The Lord will watch over your coming and going
Both now and for evermore.

Support

We all need support all through our lives – as babies and children from our parents, as teenagers and young adults from our friends, and as adults from those around us in our workplaces to help us do our jobs better. As couples we need to support each other through the ups and downs of a life together. Lack of support leads inevitably to break-ups, with widespread hurt and disillusionment.

Sometimes things happen in our lives – a death of someone close – that mean we need extra support to help us cope day to day. Trying to manage on our own can lead to breakdowns, loss of self- esteem and confidence, and loneliness.

It is so important that you seek the right support for you. You may have lost a child or your lifelong partner or a parent. You each need to be supported differently, especially if the circumstances of the death were untoward. Counselling can be very beneficial. Be advised by your G.P. as to whom to consult, Self-help groups are an excellent means of support, providing fellowship on an ongoing basis. Ask at your surgery for a list of support groups in your area – and if there are none, how about being brave enough to start one, maybe asking a friend to help? You will be surprised at how many people turn up, and it just needs to be as simple as offering tea and allowing people freedom to talk about the person they have lost, keeping within a time frame of a couple of hours max.

Thessalonians 3:1-4
We sent him to strengthen you, to encourage you in your faith...

Fear after a bereavement

I think that there are several types of fear.

One is the irrational fear, such as of spiders or wasps. I write this in September when huge spiders run across the carpet and go to who knows where in the house, while on sunny days wasps circle like miniature Great White sharks with wings, looking for someone to sting. The fear of the spider or of the wasp sting is far greater than the actual effect (unless of course you suffer anaphylactic shock as a result, in which case your fear is justified not irrational).

Another fear is the one which freezes us to the spot or which causes us sheer panic, however momentary. For example, by late summer in the first year we had achieved a new normal and were getting on with our daily lives, when I discovered that both my G.P. and my minister were to be away on their holidays at the same time – for two whole weeks! My safe world collapsed. How would I cope if something happened when the two people who 'kept me safe' were not around? I spent a few days in turmoil, imagining all sorts of scenarios. Of course, nothing bad happened, but the fear of something bad happening was very real. Also, in conversation, if I learnt that someone's child was sixteen, my heart hit the floor. I feared that at some point during their sixteenth year they too would commit suicide. Writing this, we are approaching Tom's birthday, and Alan and I will be out of the country on that day; I am fighting very hard not to panic that James will not cope on his own and will take his life. I know that that is not even a remote possibility – James will be fine– but the fear is huge. Alan and I have to learn to control that fear and not let it control us.

If you are affected like that, tell someone you trust, give voice to it, and it will not seem so huge or have such a hold over you. In our doctor's surgery is a quote by Rudyard Kipling which has helped me over many years: "I have feared many things in this life – most of which have never happened." So true!

I think that after a sudden death we are more susceptible to those sorts of fears, but even after an expected death it can be quite normal to experience these feelings of panic. It's all part of the grief process and will get less in time.

Sudden death sometimes puts fear in perspective. Possibly the worst thing in your life, or the life of one you are caring for, has already happened; so maybe our other fears, when viewed in this perspective, are not the huge mental monsters that we can make them out to be. They are often very real to the affected person and so we cannot belittle the feelings – just be prepared to listen and care and reassure.

God does not want you to be fearful, nor does He make you so. Instead, He gives us a feeling of hope.

Romans 15:13
May the God of hope fill you with all joy and peace as you trust in him, so that you may overflow with hope by the power of the Holy Spirit.

Why?

This is a natural question to ask: why did it happen? Also we can become wrapped up in ourselves and ask, why did this happen to me or to us as a family? I think this is something we can beat ourselves up about and something that can become very negative. Alan and I made a conscious decision not to think along those lines. Tom was dead – he had committed suicide, chosen death over life and nothing was going to change that – so we decided to face it, accept it and use it to help others.

Sometimes you need to ask why, if others have been involved, if due care wasn't received in hospital, if there are lessons that need to be learnt to save others, if a child was a victim of bullying etc. In those cases it is right to ask why and to seek appropriate action. But if you are asking why out of self-pity – Why me? Why us? Why now? – then it will not help your walk through grief but will only hinder you, so you will need to accept that it has happened. My G.P. told me to 'look yourself in the eye in the bathroom mirror and tell yourself that your son is dead'. This was really harsh, and to this day I have not followed this advice. I spoke the words, but I couldn't look myself in my eye – more like my chin! Yet sometimes I think I should have. I would say that the sooner you have accepted what has happened, the sooner you will be able to move on in your journey.

Another question – a huge question – is, if there is a loving God then why did He let this happen; why did He not stop it; why did He not let us find our loved one so we could have helped; why does He allow us to suffer?

All I can say is that I believe that God is the creator of all things – even you! – and that He cares for all He has made. No matter what happens to us in our lives, God is still God. He doesn't cause bad things to happen, but bad things happen anyway, sometimes as a result of the way we live our lives, sometimes through evil in this world. Yet in all the bad things that cause us pain and suffering, God is right there with us, walking with us, supporting us, carrying us when we can't walk, feeling every bit of our pain and anguish. Remember: He knows what it is like to feel as we do. He felt the same when Jesus was crucified, the Son He loved nailed to a cross for you and me. I don't know why sometimes He heals some people and not others, or why some people suffer more than others, but I do know that He is and always will be Almighty God who loves you and who longs for a loving relationship with you.

> Great is the Lord and most worthy of praise;
>> His greatness no-one can fathom.
> The Lord is gracious and compassionate,
>> slow to anger and rich in love.
> The Lord is good to all;
>> he has compassion on all he has made.
> The Lord is faithful to all his promises
>> and loving to all he has made.
> The Lord upholds all those who fall
>> and lifts up all who are bowed down.
> The Lord is righteous in all his ways
>> and loving to all he has made.
> The Lord is near to all who call on him,
>> to all who call on him in truth.
> He fulfils the desires of those who fear (love) him;
>> he hears their cry and saves them.
> The Lord watches over all who love him,
>> but the wicked he will destroy.

The key word in the above verses, taken from psalm 145, is *'all'* – and all includes you!

Epilogue

I really hope that this book has been helpful to you. I pray that you have been comforted or been able to better comfort and support others. The intention of this book has been nothing more than to share our experiences as I would if we were face to face – except that I can't hug you through a book! I pray that you have not been put off by the 'God stuff' but that you would see Him and His love for you more clearly. To find out more, why not join an Alpha course – ten weeks of fellowship, food and fun that could change your life for ever. If it were not for God's hand upon me, I would not be here to write this book for you. I pray you see that God is real.

Psalm 34:8
Taste and see that the Lord is good;
Blessed is the man who takes refuge in Him.

If you are a Christian, I pray you have been encouraged in your faith. I pray you see that you have not been abandoned by God but held securely in His hand, even in those times when you felt alone.

May the Lord bless you and keep you as you walk your journey through grief.

- Jackie -

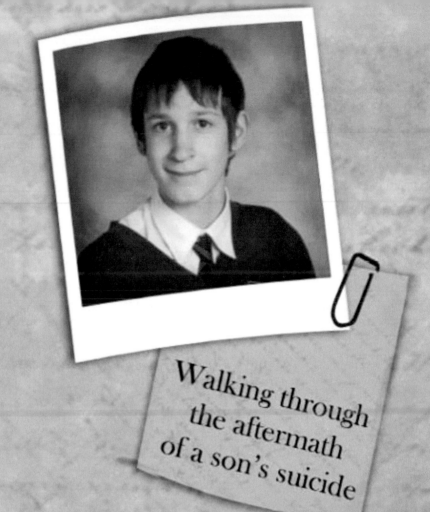

Walking through
the aftermath
of a son's suicide

Losing Tom
- Finding Grace

JACKIE SLOUGH